The Night Sky

by D.D. Maros

Scott Foresman
is an imprint of

Glenview, Illinois • Boston, Massachusetts • Mesa, Arizona
Shoreview, Minnesota • Upper Saddle River, New Jersey

Illustrators
6-7 Dan Trush; **11** David Harrington

Photographs
Every effort has been made to secure permission and provide appropriate credit for photographic material. The publisher deeply regrets any omission and pledges to correct errors called to its attention in subsequent editions.

Unless otherwise acknowledged, all photographs are the property of Pearson Education, Inc.

Photo locators denoted as follows: Top (T), Center (C), Bottom (B), Left (L), Right (R), Background (Bkgd)

CVR Chip Simons/Getty Images; **1** © Dale O'Dell/Corbis; **3** Gerard Lodriguss/Photo Researchers, Inc.; **4** The Granger Collection, NY; **5** Chip Simons/Getty Images; **8** © Dr. John D. Cunningham/Visuals Unlimited; **9** NASA/JPL; **10** Larry Landolfi/Photo Researchers, Inc.; **12** © Dale O'Dell/Corbis.

ISBN 13: 978-0-328-39438-8
ISBN 10:   0-328-39438-6

1 2 3 4 5 6 7 8 9 10 V0G1 17 16 15 14 13 12 11 10 09 08

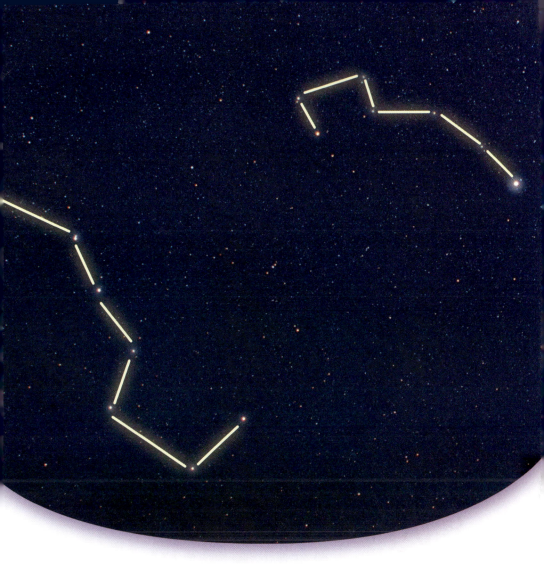

Look up.

The night sky seems to go on forever. Millions of stars shine and twinkle. Have you ever connected the stars to make a star picture?

The Ancient Greeks studied the night sky.

Pictures in the Sky

Long ago, people looked up in the night sky and saw patterns in the stars. The patterns seemed to make shapes. Ancient people gave these shapes names. Some shapes were named after animals. Some were named after people. These names are still used today.

The Big Dipper

The Big Dipper is the star shape that is easiest to find in the night sky. It is made up of seven stars that shine brightly. These seven stars form the shape of a ladle or a big spoon. That's how the Big Dipper got its name!

Big Dipper

The Big Dipper in Spring and Summer

The group of stars that make up this shape looks different from season to season. In the spring, the Big Dipper looks high in the sky. The ladle is upside-down. It could be pouring water on Earth. In the summer, the dipper looks as if it is scooping up stars!

Summer

Spring

The Big Dipper
in Fall and Winter

It is easy to see the Big Dipper in the fall. The starry ladle is right-side up. In the winter, the dipper's handle points down toward Earth. It looks like it's standing up on its handle.

No matter what time of year it is, you can always find the Big Dipper.

Winter

Fall

Polaris, the North Star

The two outer stars in the bowl of the Big Dipper are called "pointers." They both point to the North Star. The North Star is also called Polaris.

For hundreds of years, Polaris has helped travelers know which way is north.

Polaris or North Star

Polaris is like all stars. It is made up of different types of gases that burn at a very high temperature. It's the glow of the burning gases that shine in the night sky.

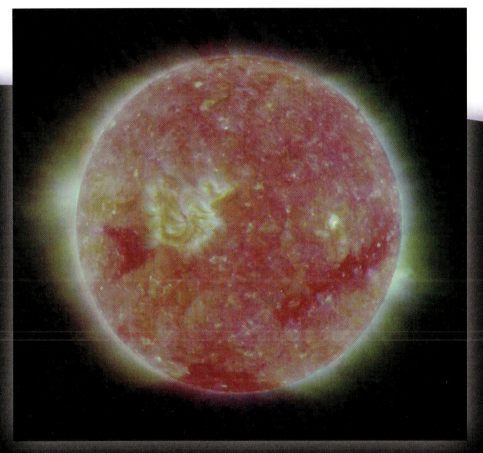

A star is made of burning gases.

The Little Dipper

The Little Dipper is harder to find than the Big Dipper. But if you can find Polaris, you should be able to find the Little Dipper. Polaris is the brightest star in the Little Dipper. It is at the end of the Little Dipper's handle. The other stars in the dipper are dim. That is why the Little Dipper can be hard to find.

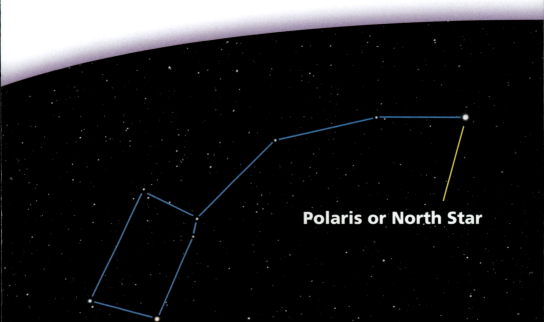

Polaris or North Star

Can you guess why this group of stars is called the Little Dipper? It has the same shape as the Big Dipper, but it is much smaller. Can you see how the Little Dipper is pouring into the Big Dipper?

Little Dipper

Big Dipper

Now you can find the Big Dipper and Polaris. You can also find the Little Dipper. You are ready to begin searching the skies for all sorts of other shapes.

Happy hunting!